Merry Christmas
Sam, Sophia and
Baby Herman!
We love you so much!
Uncle J and Aunt T

MW01097200

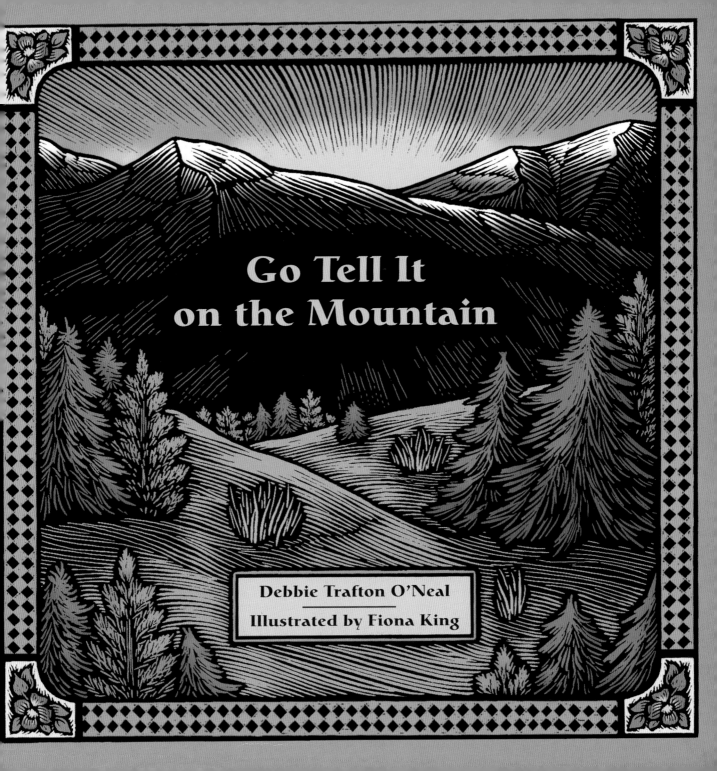

Go Tell It
on the Mountain

Debbie Trafton O'Neal

Illustrated by Fiona King

May the gift of God's Son, Jesus,
be a gift you always share with others!

Go tell it on the mountain,
Over the hills and ev'rywhere;
Go tell it on the mountain
That Jesus Christ is born!

Behold, throughout the heavens
There shone a holy light.

Go tell it on the mountain,
Over the hills and ev'rywhere;
Go tell it on the mountain
That Jesus Christ is born!

The shepherds feared and trembled
When, lo, above the earth

Go tell it on the mountain,
Over the hills and ev'rywhere;
Go tell it on the mountain
That Jesus Christ is born!

Down in a lowly manger
The humble Christ was born;

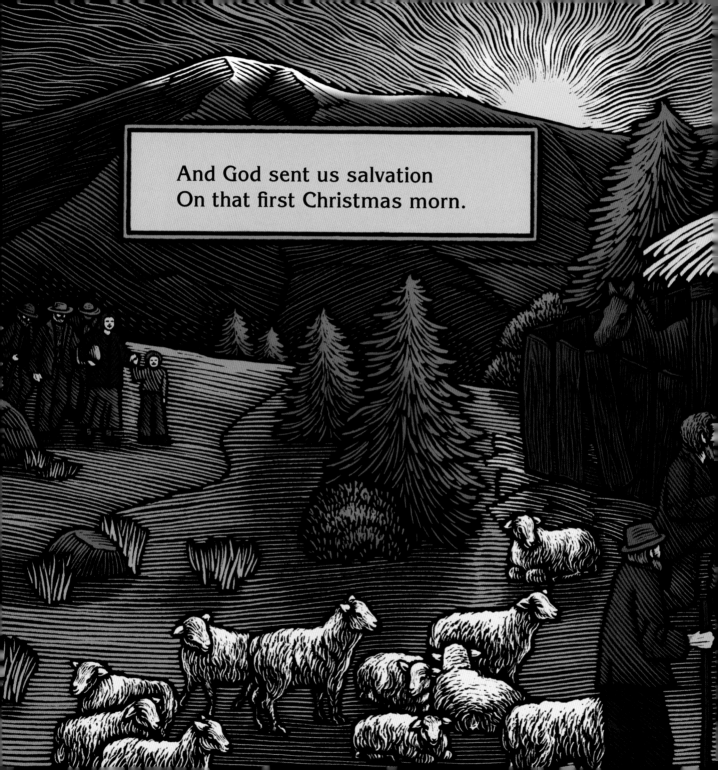

And God sent us salvation
On that first Christmas morn.

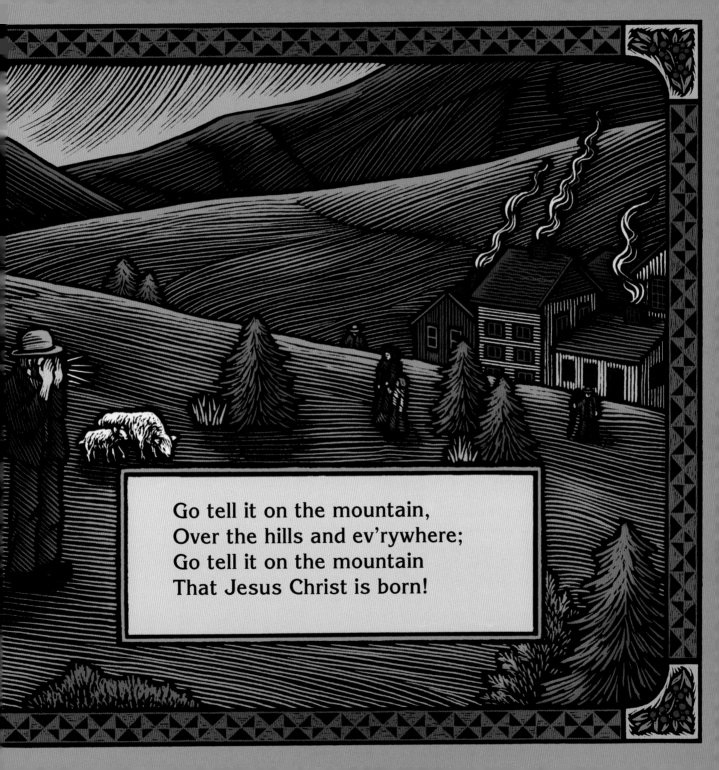

Go tell it on the mountain,
Over the hills and ev'rywhere;
Go tell it on the mountain
That Jesus Christ is born!

And as I wait for Christmas
To celebrate Christ's birth,

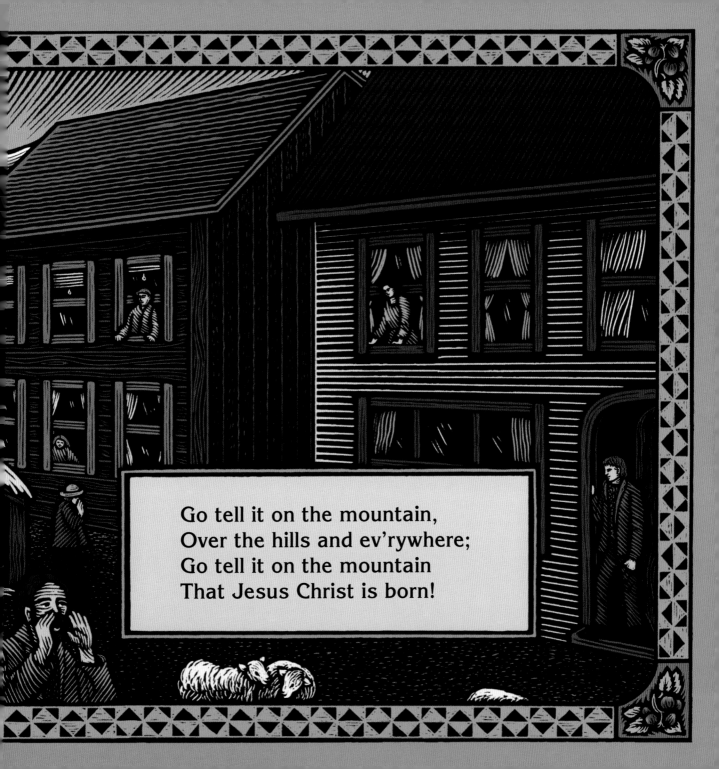

Go tell it on the mountain,
Over the hills and ev'rywhere;
Go tell it on the mountain
That Jesus Christ is born!

Christmas Family Fun

Personalize Christmas cards

Everyone loves to check the mailbox for cards, letters, and packages at Christmastime! Use one of the following ideas to make a special Christmas card and share the good news about Jesus' birth with someone you know.

❋ Take a photo of yourself surrounded by your family (don't forget pets!) and frame it with a piece of colored paper. Write a Christmas greeting on the front and a message on the back.

❋ Draw a Christmas scene and make photocopies of it on heavier paper. Use crayons or paint to color the scene and write a special Christmas message on the back. Then cut the picture into puzzle pieces, put them into envelopes, and mail them to friends. Who will be the first friend to put the puzzle together?

❋ Collect small cardboard boxes (jewelry boxes are good), and decorate these. Write good news Christmas messages on very small pieces of paper and slip one into each box. Then close, gift wrap, and deliver the boxes to friends and family members.

Jingle all the way

How do you share with people? Sometimes we share by the things we say, sometimes by the things we do. Christmas is a time for sharing. How about letting jingle bells remind you of some Christmas things to share?

Buy a large jingle bell at a craft store. Loop and tie a cord or ribbon through it to make a "good news" jingle necklace. Make one for all of your friends to wear, too. Or tie jingle bells onto your shoelaces. Everywhere you go, you will hear bells as a reminder of the good news that Jesus was born on Christmas Day!

Let your light shine

Christmas candles remind us that the light of God's love still shines, even on the darkest days of the year—and of our lives. This Christmas season (and maybe throughout the year) light a candle in your window each evening as a reminder of the light Jesus brings. Remember, never leave a burning candle unattended. Or check a local store for electric or battery-operated candles if you don't want to use wax candles.

Shout it from the rooftop

Make a family banner to hang outside your house and share the good news of Christmas with everyone who passes by. If you have a seasonal flag or banner, use it as a pattern. Cut sturdy fabric the same size as your banner, or at least 36" x 36". Plan a simple design: a shepherd's staff, a star, an angel, or several symbols that recall the first Christmas and the song, "Go Tell It on the Mountain." Cut the designs out of fabric such as felt, or use peel-and-stick vinyl, and add the shapes to your banner.

Make a 2" casing (a seam for the pole that holds the banner) on the top or side, depending on how you want to fly the banner.

Make a Christmas diorama

A diorama is a miniature scene that tells a story. It is easy to make a diorama in a shoebox, a round oatmeal box, or even a matchbox!

The box should have one removable side so that you can create the scene inside. First, decide on the story you want to show. Will it be a nighttime or daytime setting? Will it be a scene from the book *Go Tell It on the Mountain*? Or should it show part of the Christmas story? Paint or color the inside of the box to show the background: sky, mountains, village, stable, etc.

Then glue paper cutouts or miniature objects into your scene. Choose one end of the box as the "viewing" end and cut a small round peephole in the center of that end. Then punch several "spotlight holes" in the top or side of the box so that light will shine into the box on your scene.

Use the peephole and the lighting to help determine the best placement for your cutouts and other objects. When you've decided on the most effective arrangement, glue the objects into the scene. You can even hang things from the top or lid of the box with clear fishing line so that stars or angels seem to hang from the sky!

Go Tell It on the Mountain

Refrain:

Go tell it on the mountain,
Over the hills and ev'rywhere.
  Go tell it on the mountain
  That Jesus Christ is born.

Verses:

While shepherds kept their watching
O'er silent flocks by night,
  Behold throughout the heavens
  There shone a holy light.

(Sing Refrain)

The shepherds feared and trembled
When, lo, above the earth,
  Rang out the angel chorus
  Told of our Savior's birth.

(Sing Refrain)

Down in a lowly manger
The humble Christ was born.
  And God sent us salvation
  On that first Christmas morn.

(Sing Refrain)

And as I wait for Christmas
To celebrate Christ's birth,
  I want to share the good news
  With everyone on earth!

Go Tell It on the Mountain

Refrain

Go   tell it on the moun - tain,   o - ver the hills and   ev' - ry - where.

Go   tell it on the moun - tain that   Je - sus Christ is   born!

While shep-herds kept   their watch-ing o'er   si - lent flocks   by   night,
The   shep-herds feared   and   trem - bled when, lo,   a - bove   the   earth,
Down   in   a   low - ly   man - ger   the hum - ble Christ was   born.
And   as   I   wait   for Chris-tmas to   ce - le - brate Christ's birth,

to Refrain

be - hold through-out the   heav - ens there shone a   ho - ly   light.
rang out   the   an - gel   cho - rus told   of   our Sav - ior's birth.
And   God   sent   us   sal - va - tion on   that first Christ-mas   morn.
I   want to   share the   good news with ev' - ry - one on   earth!

Text: African American spiritual, refrain; John W. Work, Jr., 1871-1925, stanzas alt.; stanza 4, Debbie Tafton O'Neal
Music: GO TELL IT, African American spiritual